THE UNOFFICIAL
BIG GREEN EGG COOKBOOK

TASTY RECIPES AND STEP BY STEP DIRECTIONS TO ENJOY SMOKING WITH CERAMIC GRILL

BY ROGER MURPHY

Table of Contents

INTRODUCTION 9

WHY SMOKING..10

CHAPTER-1 BEEF...12

BEEF ROAST WITH RICH COFFEE RUB 12

BIG BEER BEEF RIBS... 15

HOT BOURBON BEEFBURGERS 17

IRISH BEEF AND POTATO STEW 19

PRIME RIB WITH FRESH HERB BUTTER 22

CHAPTER-2 PORK..24

CHORIZO-CORNBREAD STUFFED PORK CHOPS WITH SPICY CREMA
.... 24

HERBY PORK ROULADE 27

SPICY KOREAN PORK BULGOGI 29

STICKY PEACH-WHISKEY GLAZED PORK BELLY 33

SWEET AND SMOKY PULLED PORK SANDWICHES 36

CHAPTER-3 HAM 39

GRILLED AND GLAZED HOLIDAY HAM WITH PINEAPPLE...............39

ORANGE-MUSTARD GLAZED GRILLED HAM 41

SMOKED BONE-IN HAM WITH JALAPENO-PEACH GLAZE..............43

SMOKED HAM WITH ROOT BEER GLAZE 46

CHAPTER-4 LAMB.. 49

GARLIC AND HERB RACK OF LAMB...49

LAMB WITH HOMEMADE MINT SAUCE...51

MEDITERRANEAN LAMB AND FETA BURGERS............................54

SAGE-RUBBED LAMB CHOPS...56

SPICY LAMB SKEWERS 58

CHAPTER-5 FISH 61

HONEY-GLAZED PECAN SMOKED HALIBUT 61

JOHN DORY WITH OYSTER CREAM, APPLE AND PARSLEY JUICE 64

LEMON AND ROSEMARY MARINATED GROUPER WITH TOMATO-
BASIL SAUCE 68

CHAPTER-6 SEAFOOD.. 71

CRAB CAKES WITH SWEET BBQ RANCH DIPPING SAUCE 71

OYSTER SPAGHETTI 74

RED CHILI SCALLOPS WITH HOMEMADE SALSA............................ 77

CHAPTER-7 CHICKEN...80

GREEK HERB ROASTED CHICKEN 80

RANCH-ROSEMARY CHICKEN KEBABS 83

SPANISH-SPICED BEER CAN CHICKEN 85

CHAPTER-8 TURKEY 88

APPLE, BOURBON, AND BACON STUFFED TURKEY 88

CLASSIC ROAST TURKEY 91

TURKEY PARMIGIANA.. 93

CHAPTER-9 GAME 95

CHERRY-SMOKED VENISON LOIN WITH PINK PEPPERCORNS 95

CHILI-CRUSTED COLA WILD BOAR HAM 98

SMOKED DUCK BREAST WITH FRUIT 100

CHAPTER-10 VEGGIES..103

DOUBLE-SMOKED BACON STUFFED POTATOES......................... 103

MASHED SMOKED AUBERGINE 106

TRIO OF MUSHROOM SALAD WITH TOMATO PERSILLADE 109

CHAPTER-11 SMOKING TIPS AND TRICKS 112

Selecting a Smoker 112

Choose your wood...113

Select the right meat 115

Find the right temperature 115

The core difference between cold and hot smoking 116

The basic preparations 117

The core elements of smoking!....................................118

CONCLUSION 119

MY BOOKS 120

Get Your FREE Gift 129

INTRODUCTION

The ultimate how-to guide for smoking all types of pork, beef, ham, vegetables, fish poultry, and game. This book on smoking meats for beginners is the guide to mastering the low and slow art of smoking meats at your home. This guide is an essential book for beginners who want to smoke meat without needing expert help from others. This book offers detailed guidance obtained by years of smoking meat, includes clear instructions and step-by-step directions for every recipe. This is the only guide you will ever need to professionally smoke a variety of meat. From well-known beef brisket, pork ribs the book includes delicate turkey, venison, chicken, and pheasant smoked meat recipes. The book includes full-color photographs of every finished meal to make your job easier. Whether you are a beginner meat smoker or looking to go beyond the basics, the book gives you the tools and tips you need to start that perfectly smoked meat.

WHY SMOKING

Smoking is generally used as one of the cooking methods nowadays. The food enriches in protein such as meat would spoil quickly, if cooked for a longer period of time with modern cooking techniques. Whereas, Smoking is a low & slow process of cooking the meat. Where there is a smoke, there is a flavor. With white smoke, you can boost the flavor of your food. In addition to this statement, you can preserve the nutrition present in the food as well. This is flexible & one of the oldest techniques of making food. It's essential for you to brush the marinade over your food while you cook and let the miracle happen. The only thing you need to do is to add a handful of fresh coals or wood chips as and when required. Just taste your regular grilled meat and a smoked meat, you yourself would find the difference. Remember one thing i.e. "Smoking is an art". With a little time & practice, even you can become an expert. Once you become an expert with smoking technique, believe me, you would never look for other cooking techniques. To find one which smoking technique works for you, you must experiment with different woods & cooking methods. Just cook the meat over indirect heat source & cook it for hours. When smoking your meats, it's very important that you let the smoke to escape & move around.

CHAPTER-1 BEEF

BEEF ROAST WITH RICH COFFEE RUB

(TOTAL COOK TIME 26 HOURS 15 MINUTES)

INGREDIENTS FOR 4 SERVINGS

THE MEAT

- Beef chuck roast (4-lb, 1.8-kgs)
- Olive oil
- Black pepper
- Salted butter, melted

THE RUB

- Onion powder – 1 tablespoon
- Smoked paprika – 2 tablespoons
- Garlic powder – 1 tablespoon
- Chili powder – 1 teaspoon
- Mustard powder – 1 teaspoon
- Oregano – 1 teaspoon
- Coriander – 1 teaspoon
- White sugar – 1 teaspoon
- Dried thyme – 1 teaspoon
- Salt – 1 tablespoon
- Brown sugar – 2 tablespoons
- Ground coffee – ¾ cup

THE SMOKE

- When you are ready to cook, preheat your EGG to 275° F (135°C) using your wood of choice and prepare for direct cooking.

METHOD

1. First, prepare the rub. Combine the onion powder along with the paprika, garlic, chili, mustard, oregano, coriander, white sugar, thyme, salt, brown sugar, and coffee in a small bowl.
2. Brush the roast all over with oil and season with black pepper. Cover the outside of the roast evenly with the prepared rub. Cover and chill for 24 hours.
3. Allow the meat to come to room temperature before cooking.
4. Arrange the meat on one side of the hot grill and cook for approximately 1½ hours or until the meat registers an internal temperature of 125°F (50°C).
5. Baste the cooked meat with melted butter, tent with aluminum foil and set aside for half an hour before slicing and serving.
6. Enjoy.

BIG BEER BEEF RIBS

(TOTAL COOK TIME 6 HOURS 15 MINUTES)

INGREDIENTS FOR 4 SERVINGS

THE MEAT

- 1 rack beef short ribs (6-lb, 2.7-kgs)

THE INGREDIENTS

- Olive oil
- Salt and black pepper – to taste
- Garlic powder – 1 tablespoon
- 1 bottle stout beer

THE SMOKE

- Preheat your EGG to 265° F (130°C) using a small amount of oak wood and prepare for indirect cooking.

METHOD

1. Carefully peel away the membrane from the bone side of the ribs.
2. Brush the entire rack with olive oil and season well with salt, black pepper, and garlic.
3. Arrange the ribs on the grate so they are bone side facing down and grill for a couple of hours before flipping and grilling for a further hour. They should be a rich gold-brown.
4. Transfer the rack to a disposable aluminum pan and pour over the stout beer. Cover securely with aluminum foil and place back on the grill. Cook for another few hours or until the meat registers an internal temperature of 200°F (93°C).
5. Cut the rack into individual bones before serving.

HOT BOURBON BEEFBURGERS

(TOTAL COOK TIME 25 MINUTES)

INGREDIENTS FOR 4 SERVINGS

THE MEAT

- Ground beef (1-lb, 0.45-kgs)

THE INGREDIENTS

- Onion soup mix – 2 tablespoons
- Worcestershire sauce – 2 tablespoons
- Bourbon – 2 tablespoons
- Hot sauce – 1 teaspoon
- 4 brioche buns, toasted

THE SMOKE

- Preheat your EGG to 375° F (190°C) using your wood of choice and prepare for direct cooking.

METHOD

1. In a large bowl, using clean hands, combine the beef, soup mix, Worcestershire sauce, bourbon, and hot sauce.
2. Shape the mixture into 4 equally-sized patties and make a small indent in the center of each.
3. Place directly on the grill and cook for 5 minutes on each side until medium-rare.
4. Serve the burgers inside the buns straight away.

IRISH BEEF AND POTATO STEW

(TOTAL COOK TIME 26 HOURS 15 MINUTES)

INGREDIENTS FOR 8 SERVINGS

THE MEAT

- Boneless beef chuck roast, cubed (3-lb, 1.35-kgs)

THE STEW

- Beef seasoning blend – 3 tablespoons
- Vegetable oil – 4 tablespoons
- 3 celery stalks, chopped
- 2 yellow onions, peeled and chopped
- Tomato paste – 1 tablespoon
- All-purpose flour – 3 tablespoons
- Minced garlic – 1 tablespoon
- Fresh thyme, chopped – 2 teaspoons
- Salt – 1 teaspoon
- Black pepper – ¾ teaspoon
- Beef broth – 1 cup
- Irish stout beer – 2½ cups
- 4 turnips, peeled and cubed
- 4 potatoes, peeled and cubed
- 3 carrots, peeled and chopped
- Fresh parsley, chopped – ¼ cup

THE GRILL

- Preheat your EGG to 350° F (175°C) and prepare for direct cooking.

METHOD

1. Arrange a Dutch oven directly onto the grill grate to preheat.

2. Sprinkle beef seasoning over the cubes of meat and toss to coat.

3. Add 2 tablespoons of oil to the Dutch oven and wait until it begins to smoke.

4. Add the beef and cook for 10 minutes until browned on all sides. Set the meat to one side.

5. Add the remaining oil to the Dutch oven along with the celery and onion. Cook for 10 minutes until softened.

6. Stir in the tomato paste, flour, garlic, thyme, salt, and black pepper and cook for 60 seconds.

7. Pour in the beef broth and stout beer, stir well to combine.

8. Return the meat to the pot. Cover with a lid and cook for 45 minutes.

9. Add the turnips, potatoes, and carrots and cook, covered, for another 1½-2 hours until the beef and vegetables are tender.

10. Stir in the parsley, serve and enjoy.

PRIME RIB WITH FRESH HERB BUTTER

(TOTAL COOK TIME 26 HOURS 15 MINUTES)

INGREDIENTS FOR 8 SERVINGS

THE MEAT

- Boneless rib-eye roast (5-lb, 2.25-kgs)
- Salt and black pepper

THE BUTTER

- Butter, softened – 1 cup
- Fresh thyme, chopped – ¼ cup
- 4 garlic cloves, peeled and crushed
- Fresh parsley, chopped – ¼ cup
- Fresh tarragon, chopped – ¼ cup

THE SMOKE

- Preheat your EGG to 325° F (165°C) using your wood of choice and prepare for indirect cooking.

METHOD

1. Season the beef liberally with salt and black pepper.
2. Next, prepare the butter. Combine the softened butter, fresh thyme, garlic, parsley, and tarragon in a small bowl until smooth and fluffy. Evenly spread the butter over the outside of the beef.
3. Place the beef on the grate and cook for approximately 1½-2 hours until the meat registers an internal temperature of 125°F (50°C).
4. Transfer the cooked meat to a serving platter, tent loosely with aluminum foil and set aside for 15-20 minutes to rest.
5. Slice thickly and serve.

CHAPTER-2 PORK

CHORIZO-CORNBREAD STUFFED PORK CHOPS WITH SPICY CREMA

(TOTAL COOK TIME 1 HOUR)

INGREDIENTS FOR 4 SERVINGS

THE MEAT

- 4 double-cut pork chops

THE SPICY CREMA

- Sour cream – ½ cup
- Adobo sauce – 1 teaspoon

THE STUFFING

- Olive oil – 1 tablespoon
- Sweet and smoky seasoning mix – 4 tablespoons
- Cornbread crumbled – 1 cup
- Smoked chorizo, chopped
- Fresh cilantro, chopped - ½ cup
- Chicken stock – ½ cup

THE GRILL

- Preheat your EGG to 450° F (230°C) and prepare for direct cooking.

METHOD

1. First, make the spicy crema. Stir together the sour cream and adobo sauce in a small bowl and chill until ready to use.
2. Use a sharp knife to cut a 2-ins (5.0-cm) pocket in each pork chop. Brush each chop with olive oil and sprinkle each one with 1 tablespoon of the rub.
3. Next, prepare the stuffing. Combine the crumbled cornbread, chorizo, cilantro and stock in a bowl. Stuff the mixture evenly into the pocket of each pork chop.
4. Arrange the chops on the grill and close the lid. Cook for a few minutes on each side. Close the bottom and top vents and cook for another 15 minutes until the meat registers an internal temperature of 145°F (65°C).
5. Serve the pork chops with the spicy crema.

HERBY PORK ROULADE

(TOTAL COOK TIME 1 HOURS 25 MINUTES)

INGREDIENTS FOR 8 SERVINGS

THE MEAT

- 1 pork neck (4.5-lb, 2-kgs)
- Sea salt

THE HERBS

- 1 bunch fresh marjoram
- 1 bunch fresh lovage

- Sea salt
- 1 garlic bulb, peeled and chopped

THE SMOKE

- When ready to cook, preheat your EGG to 430° F (220°C) using charcoal and prepare for direct cooking.

METHOD

1. First, prepare the herbs. Pick the leaves from the marjoram and lovage and finely chop.
2. Arrange the pork neck on a clean chopping board. Measure 1.2-ins (3-cm) up from the bottom of the neck and make a lengthwise incision. Roll the top part of the meat over and keep cutting lengthwise until you have a rectangular piece of meat with an even 1.2-ins (3.0-cm) thickness.
3. Sprinkle the herbs over the pork and season with sea salt and garlic.
4. Starting from the short side, roll up the meat and secure with kitchen twine.
5. Place the meat on the grill and close the lid, cook for approximately an hour rolling the roulade every 5 minutes so that it cooks evenly.
6. The meat is ready when it registers an internal temperature of 140°F (60°C).
7. Allow the roulade to rest for 15-20 minutes tented with aluminum foil.
8. Slice and serve.

SPICY KOREAN PORK BULGOGI

(TOTAL COOK TIME 5 HOURS)

INGREDIENTS FOR 4 SERVINGS

THE MEAT

- 1 pork neck (1.3-lb, 0.6-kgs)
- Sunflower oil – 4 tablespoons

THE MARINADE

- 1 shallot, peeled and chopped
- 1 Asian pear, peeled, cored and quartered
- Chunk fresh ginger, peeled and chopped – 0.8-ins (2-cm)
- 2 garlic cloves, peeled and chopped
- Korean chili paste – 3 tablespoons
- 2 spring onions, sliced
- Mirin – 2 tablespoons
- Soy sauce – 3 tablespoons
- Korean chili flakes – 2 tablespoons
- Cane sugar – 3 tablespoons
- Toasted sesame seeds – 1 tablespoon
- Black pepper – 1 teaspoon

THE SAUCE

- 2 spring onions, sliced
- Korean soybean paste – 4 tablespoons
- Korean chili paste – 2 tablespoons
- Sugar – 1 tablespoon
- Toasted sesame seeds – 1 tablespoon
- Sesame oil – 2 tablespoons
- 2 garlic cloves, peeled and grated

THE SMOKE

- When ready to cook, ignite lump charcoal in your EGG and preheat to 390° F (200°C), prepare for direct cooking. Place a cast iron skillet on the grill grate to preheat.

METHOD

1. First, prepare the marinade. Add the shallot, pear, ginger, garlic, chili paste, spring onions, mirin, soy sauce, chili flakes, cane sugar, sesame seeds, and black pepper to a food processor and blitz to a smooth paste and transfer to a large bowl.

2. Slice the pork into 6 equal pieces and arrange in the bowl along with the marinade. Turn the meat to coat it well and evenly.

3. Cover with kitchen plastic wrap and chill in the fridge for between 3-4 hours.

4. In the meantime, prepare the sauce. Combine the spring onion, soybean paste, and chili paste in a bowl. Sprinkle over the sugar and sesame seeds. Slowly pour over the sesame oil and sprinkle over the grated garlic. Cover with plastic wrap and chill until ready to use.

5. Remove the meat from the marinade and pat away any excess. Reserve the marinade for later use.

6. Add the sunflower oil to the preheated skillet.

7. Arrange half of the sliced pork in the skillet, close the lid and cook for 6-7 minutes on each side. Take the meat out of the skillet and repeat with the remaining slices.

8. Add the reserved marinade to the skillet, close the grill id and bring the marinade to a simmer until hot through and thickened.

9. Cut the cooked meat into strips and toss in the marinade.

10. Serve alongside the prepared sauce.

STICKY PEACH-WHISKEY GLAZED PORK BELLY

(TOTAL COOK TIME 3 HOURS)

INGREDIENTS FOR 6 SERVINGS

THE MEAT

- Pork belly (1.75-lb, 0.8-kgs)

THE RUB

- Thyme – 2 tablespoons
- Smoked paprika – 6 tablespoons
- Onion powder – 1 tablespoon
- Garlic powder – 1 tablespoon
- Brown sugar – 2 tablespoons
- Black pepper – 1 tablespoon
- Ginger – 1 tablespoon
- Pinch chili powder
- Agave nectar
- Sea salt

THE GLAZE

- BBQ sauce – ½ cup
- Peach preserves – 1 cup
- Agave nectar – 3 tablespoons
- Bourbon whiskey – 3 tablespoons
- Floral honey – 3 tablespoons

THE SMOKE

- Preheat your EGG to 325° F (190°C) and prepare for indirect cooking. Scatter a handful of pecan smoking chips over the charcoal embers.

METHOD

1. First, prepare the rub. Combine the thyme, paprika, onion powder, garlic powder, sugar, black pepper, ginger, and chili powder in a small bowl.

2. Slice away the majority of the pork's fat layer leaving just ⅛-ins (3.5-mm) remaining. Slice the remaining soft white fat crosswise.

3. Cover the meat with ⅔ of the prepared rub, drizzle with agave nectar and season with sea salt.

4. Arrange the meat, fat-side upwards, on the grill grid and close the lid. Smoke the meat for just over 35 minutes.

5. In the meantime, prepare the glaze. Place a pan over moderately high heat and add the BBQ sauce, peach preserves, agave nectar, whiskey, and honey. Stir well to combine and bring the mixture to a boil. Turn the heat down to low and simmer for 10 minutes until thickened and sticky.

6. Brush ⅔ of the glaze mixture over the pork and continue to cook until the meat registers an internal temperature of 165°F (75°C).

7. Set the meat to one side, tented in foil, and increase the temperature of the smoker/grill to 375°F (190°C).

8. Slice the meat into 0.5-ins (4.0-cm) cubes and arrange in a cast-iron griddle. Pour over the remaining glaze and sprinkle over the remaining rub. Arrange the griddle back on the grill and cook for several minutes until the glaze is sticky and the meat hot through.

9. Serve and enjoy.

SWEET AND SMOKY PULLED PORK SANDWICHES

(TOTAL COOK TIME 14 HOURS 30 MINUTES)

INGREDIENTS FOR 18 SERVINGS

THE MEAT

- 1 pork neck (5.5-lb, 2.5-kgs)

THE RUB

- Brown sugar – 10 tablespoons
- Onion powder – 3 tablespoons
- Turmeric – 2 tablespoons
- Cayenne pepper – 1½ tablespoons
- Garlic powder – 3 tablespoons
- Salt – 7 tablespoons
- Paprika – 7 tablespoons

THE SANDWICHES

- BBQ sauce
- 18 soft rolls
- Coleslaw, for serving

THE SMOKE

- Soak a large handful of cherry wood in water. Add a few handfuls of unsoaked cherry wood to the unlit charcoal. Open the draft door and arrange three fire starters over the charcoal and light. Keep the lid open for 10 minutes.
- Sprinkle the soaked cherry wood over the now-glowing charcoal. Set up the convector and arrange a grid inside.

METHOD

1. First, prepare the rub. Combine the sugar, onion powder, turmeric, cayenne pepper, garlic powder, salt, and paprika.
2. Cover the outside of the meat with the rub.
3. Arrange the pork on the grid and heat the EGG to a temperature of 220°F (105°C). Cook the pork for approximately 8 hours until it registers an internal temperature of 160°F (70°C).
4. Remove the meat from the grill and wrap in aluminum foil. Return to the grill and cook for another several hours until it registers an internal temperature of 195°F (90°C).
5. Take the meat off the grill and allow to rest in the foil for another few hours.
6. Shred the cooled pork and toss in BBQ sauce.
7. Serve inside soft rolls topped with coleslaw.

CHAPTER-3 HAM

GRILLED AND GLAZED HOLIDAY HAM WITH PINEAPPLE

(TOTAL COOK TIME 3 HOURS 20 MINUTES)

INGREDIENTS FOR 20 SERVINGS

THE HAM

- 1 bone-in ham (10-lb, 4.5-kgs)

THE GLAZE

- Honey – 1 cup
- White Zinfandel wine – ½ cup
- Zest and fresh juice of 1 medium orange
- Brown sugar – 3 cups
- 1 can crushed pineapple (20-oz, 567-gms)
- 1 fresh pineapple, cored, sliced into rings

THE SMOKE

- Set the EGG for indirect cooking to 225°F (110°C)
- Position the plate setter over the charcoal
- Use a drip pan
- Choose wood chips of choice

METHOD

1. In a bowl, combine the honey with the wine, orange zest and juice, and brown sugar. Stir to incorporate.
2. Grill the ham for approximately 3- 3½ hours in total, glazing every half an hour.
3. For the final 30 minutes or when the ham registers an internal temperature of 120°F (40°C), using toothpicks attach the pineapple rings to the ham.
4. The ham is cooked when it reaches an internal temperature of 140°F (60°C).

ORANGE-MUSTARD GLAZED GRILLED HAM

(TOTAL COOK TIME 3 HOURS 45 MINUTES)

INGREDIENTS FOR 18-20 SERVINGS

THE HAM

- 1 spiral sliced cooked ham, pre-cooked (10-lb, 4.5-kgs)

THE RUB

- Dijon mustard
- Spicy rub, of choice

THE GLAZE

- Orange marmalade – ½ cup
- Dijon mustard – ¼ cup
- Soy sauce – 2 tablespoons
- Hot sauce, to taste

THE SMOKE

- Light the charcoal and heat for 10-15 minutes.
- Position the plate setter with the feet up, position a pan on top and fill with grapefruit flavor beer. Add the grill grate.
- Adjust both the bottom and top vents and maintain a temperature of 250°F (120°C).
- Use peach wood chips, adding additional chips as needed.

METHOD

1. Liberally spread the mustard over the ham and generously coat with the rub.
2. Smoke the ham for 20-30 minutes per pound.
3. In a bowl, combine the orange marmalade with the mustard, and soy sauce. Taste and add hot sauce as needed.
4. Brush the glaze onto the ham and continue to cook for half an hour.
5. Remove the ham from the EGG and serve.

SMOKED BONE-IN HAM WITH JALAPENO-PEACH GLAZE

(TOTAL COOK TIME 3 HOURS 20 MINUTES)

INGREDIENTS FOR 6 SERVINGS

THE HAM

- 1 bone-in ham (10-lb, 4.5-kgs)
- BBQ of choice - 2-3 tablespoons

THE GLAZE

- Unsalted butter – 1 tablespoon
- Jalapeno, diced, seeded – 1 tablespoon
- Garlic, peeled, minced – 1 teaspoon
- Fresh ginger root, peeled, sliced 1-ins (2.5-cms)
- Freshly squeezed orange juice – ½ cup
- Jar of peach preserves (13-ozs, 368-gms)

THE GRILL

- Heat your EGG to 275°F (135°C).

METHOD

1. First, with a sharp knife score the fat on the ham in a diamond pattern.
2. Season the ham all over with a BBQ seasoning of choice.
3. Position the ham on the smoker and cook for 12-15 minutes per pound, until it reaches an internal temperature of 135°F (57°C).
4. While the ham smokes, prepare the glaze.
5. Over moderate heat, in a pan, combine the butter with the jalapeno and cook for approximately 2-3 minutes.
6. Add the garlic and cook until golden, for 2 minutes.
7. Add the ginger and cook for an additional couple of minutes.
8. Pour in the orange juice to deglaze the pan and cook until the liquid reduces by half.
9. Whisk in the peach preserves and bring to a light boil, before simmering until thickened, for approximately 5 minutes.
10. When the ham registers its desired internal temperature of 135°F (57°C) brush it all over with the glaze and continue smoking until it registers 145°F (62°C).
11. Remove the ham from the EGG, slice and serve with a bowl of the glaze on the side.

SMOKED HAM WITH ROOT BEER GLAZE

(TOTAL COOK TIME 6 HOUR 15 MINUTES)

INGREDIENTS FOR 12-16 SERVINGS

THE HAM

- 1 smoked spiral sliced ham (10-lb, 4.5-kgs)

THE GLAZE

- Sweet cream butter – ½ cup
- Pinch sea salt
- Sweet heat rub – 2 tablespoons
- Light brown sugar – ½ cup
- Root beer, any brand (6-oz, 170-gms)

THE INGREDIENTS

- Sweet-spicy BBQ rub
- 1 cup fresh apple juice

THE SMOKE

- Set your EGG for indirect cooking at 300°F (148°C).
- Use apple wood chips on top of the charcoal and combine.
- Position the plate setting with the grilling grate on top.

METHOD

1. To prepare the glaze: In a small pan, melt the butter.
2. Add a pinch of salt along with the sweet heat rub, light brown sugar, and root beer. Stir until the sugar is entirely dissolved and use to glaze the ham, as directed.
3. Remove the ham from its packaging and set on the side.
4. Generously season with the sweet rub.
5. Position the ham face downward on the wire rack and into the pan.
6. Pour the apple juice or water into the pan, but not over the ham.
7. Allow to marinate for 60 minutes.
8. Set the ham on the smoker and smoke.
9. Glaze the ham when it reaches an internal temperature of 120°F (50°C).
10. Continue to smoke until the internal heat registers 140°F (60°C). The total smoking time is approximately 4 hours.
11. Remove the ham from the smoker and loosely cover with aluminum foil, before setting aside to rest for half an hour.
12. Slice, serve and enjoy.

CHAPTER-4 LAMB

GARLIC AND HERB RACK OF LAMB

(TOTAL COOK TIME 45 MINUTES)

INGREDIENTS FOR 4 SERVINGS

THE MEAT

- 2 racks of lamb

THE INGREDIENTS

- ½ bunch fresh rosemary, needles removed
- ½ bunch fresh thyme leaves chopped
- 6 garlic cloves, peeled and minced
- Sea salt
- Mustard

THE GRILL

- Preheat your EGG to 355°F (180°C) and prepare for direct cooking.

METHOD

1. Combine the herbs (rosemary and thyme), garlic, and sea salt on a chopping board.
2. Brush a thin layer of mustard over the outside of the racks then evenly coat in the herb mixture.
3. Arrange the lamb on the grill, close the lid and cook for 8 minutes, making quarter turns every 2 minutes.
4. Allow the lamb to cook for another 15 minutes until the meat registers an internal temperature of 120°F (50°C).
5. Take the lamb racks off the grill and cover loosely with foil, allow to rest for several minutes before serving.

LAMB WITH HOMEMADE MINT SAUCE

(TOTAL COOK TIME 3 HOURS 25 MINUTES)

INGREDIENTS FOR 4 SERVINGS

THE MEAT

- 8-10 bone rack of lamb

THE MINT SAUCE

- Fresh mint leaves – 1 cup
- White wine vinegar – 2 tablespoons
- Olive oil – ¾ cup
- Sea salt – 1 teaspoon
- Fresh lemon juice – 1 tablespoon
- Black pepper – ½ teaspoon

THE RUB

- Dijon mustard – 2½ tablespoons
- 2 garlic cloves, peeled and minced
- Fresh mint, chopped – 2 tablespoons
- Onion powder – 1 teaspoon
- Sea salt – 1¼ teaspoons
- Black pepper – ½ teaspoon
- Olive oil – ¼ cup

THE GRILL

- When ready to cook, preheat your EGG to 500°F (260°C) and prepare for direct cooking.

METHOD

1. First, prepare the mint sauce. Add the mint, vinegar, oil, salt, lemon juice, and black pepper to a blender and blitz until combined. Chill until ready to serve.
2. Next, prepare the rub. Combine the mustard, garlic, mint, and onion powder in a small bowl.
3. Season the lamb with salt and black pepper, then evenly brush with the mustard mixture.
4. Transfer the meat to a ziplock bag and pour in the oil. Rub the lamb to coat in the oil. Arrange in a bowl and chill for a few hours.
5. Allow the lamb to come to room temperature before grilling.
6. Cover the exposed bones with aluminum foil and arrange the lamb directly on the grill. Close the lid and cook for several minutes before flipping and cooking for a final 5 minutes. Take off the grill, cover loosely with foil and allow to rest for several minutes before serving with the mint sauce.

MEDITERRANEAN LAMB AND FETA BURGERS

(TOTAL COOK TIME 30 MINUTES)

INGREDIENTS FOR 4 SERVINGS

THE MEAT

- Ground lamb (2-lb, 0.9-kgs)
- Ground beef (1-lb, 0.45-kgs)

THE INGREDIENTS

- Feta, crumbled – ½ cup
- BBQ rub – 1 tablespoon
- 4 brioche buns, toasted

THE GRILL

- Preheat your EGG to 500°F (260°C) and prepare for direct cooking.

METHOD

1. Combine the ground meat (lamb and beef), feta, and BBQ rub in a bowl.
2. Using clean hands, form the mixture into 4 equal patties. Make a thumb-sized indent in the center of each patty.
3. Arrange the patties on the grill and cook for a couple of minutes on each side. Close the vents and cook for another 5 minutes.
4. Allow the patties to rest for several minutes before serving inside the buns.

SAGE-RUBBED LAMB CHOPS

(TOTAL COOK TIME 8 HOURS 25 MINUTES)

INGREDIENTS FOR 4 SERVINGS

THE MEAT

- Lamb rib chops (2-lb, 0.9-kgs)

THE RUB

- Fresh sage (8-oz, 225-gms)
- 2 garlic cloves
- 4 sprigs thyme
- Olive oil – 6 tablespoons
- Pinch salt and black pepper
- Butter

THE GRILL

- When ready to cook, preheat your EGG to 300°F (150°C) arrange a cast iron skillet on the grid to get nice and hot.

METHOD

1. Using clean hands pulverize and crush the sage to release its oils.
2. Place the sage, garlic, and thyme in the base of a large bowl. Lay the lamb on top, drizzle over the oil and season well with salt and black pepper. Toss to combine. Cover tightly with plastic wrap and chill overnight.
3. Arrange the lamb in the skillet along with a knob of butter and baste while cooking until the lamb is medium rare, 120°F (50°C).
4. Allow to rest for several minutes, tented with aluminum foil, before serving.

SPICY LAMB SKEWERS

(TOTAL COOK TIME 40 MINUTES)

INGREDIENTS FOR 6-8 SERVINGS

THE MEAT

- 1 lamb roast (2-lb, 0.9-kgs)

THE RUB

- Cumin seeds – 3 tablespoons
- Black peppercorns – 1 tablespoon
- Dried chili flakes – 1 tablespoon
- Salt – 1 tablespoon
- Onion powder – ½ teaspoons
- Garlic powder – ½ teaspoon

THE SMOKE

- For direct cooking, set your EGG to 450°F (232°C).
- When the temperature is stable, oil the grill grates before cooking the kebabs.
- With long-handled BBQ tongs dip folded kitchen paper towels in cooking oil and carefully wipe the grill gates down, making a minimum of three good passes to make a nonstick surface.

METHOD

1. In a frying pan, toast the cumin seeds along with the peppercorns for 1-2 minutes. Move the cumin seeds around the frying pan to ensure even toasting.

2. As soon as the seeds and peppercorns are fragrant remove them from the heat and transfer to a coffee or spice grinder, and on a moderate setting, pulverize.

3. Transfer the ground mixture to a bowl and add the remaining spice rub ingredients; chili flakes, salt, onion powder, and garlic powder.

4. Cut the lamb into 1.25-ins (2.18-cms) and place them in a large mixing bowl.

5. Add the spice rub to the bowl and toss to evenly coat all of the lamb. Put to one side for approximately 15 minutes.

6. Thread the cubes of lamb onto skewers, aiming for between 6-8 pieces per skewer.

7. Arrange the kebabs on the grill and cook for between 10-12 minutes, turning every 2-3 minutes.

8. Remove the kebabs from the grill and serve.

CHAPTER-5 FISH

HONEY-GLAZED PECAN SMOKED HALIBUT

(TOTAL COOK TIME 3 HOURS 5 MINS)

INGREDIENTS FOR 4 SERVINGS

THE FISH

- 4 halibut filets
- Pecan rub
- Clover honey, warm – 4 tablespoons

THE BRINE

- Kosher salt – ½ cup
- Sugar – 1 cup
- Cumin – 4 tablespoons
- White pepper – 1 tablespoon
- 2 bay leaves, crushed
- Water – 1 gallon

THE SMOKE

- For indirect cooking, set your EGG to 275°F (135°C) using pecan smoking chips.

METHOD

1. To prepare the brine: Combine the kosher salt with the sugar, cumin, white pepper, bay leaves, and water and mix until entirely dissolved.

2. Pour the brine over the halibut filets and set aside for 2 hours.

3. Remove the halibut from the brine, rinse and using kitchen paper towel, pat dry.

4. Season on both sides with the pecan rub.

5. Skin side facing down arrange the fish filets directly on the cooking grate. The skin is easily removed after cooking.

6. Smoke the fish until an internal thermometer registers 135°F (57°C). The smoke will take approximately half an hour at 275°F (135°C).

7. Drizzle the fish with warm honey 10 minutes before it's done cooking.

8. Using a spatula, carefully remove the fish, set aside to rest for several minutes and serve.

JOHN DORY WITH OYSTER CREAM, APPLE AND PARSLEY JUICE

(TOTAL COOK TIME 1 HOUR 35 MINS)

INGREDIENTS FOR 4 SERVINGS

THE FISH

- 2 John Dory fish fillets heads off (2-lb, 0.9-kgs each)
- Salt, to season
- Olive oil, to season
- 4 fresh oysters, unopened

THE INGREDIENTS

- Kohlrabi apple and parsley juice, see recipe
- Oyster cream, see recipe
- Herbs of choice, to serve
- Borage flowers, to garnish

THE JUICE

- Juice and leaves of 1 green kohlrabi or German turnip
- Juice of 2 Granny Smith apples
- Parsley (10-oz, 285-gms)
- Water – 1 cup
- Cornstarch, optional
- Salt, to season

THE OYSTER CREAM

- 12 oysters, unopened
- Cream – $2_{1/8}$ cups
- Gelatin – 2 teaspoons

THE GRILL

- Prepare your EGG for direct cooking and preheat to 650°F (345°C) with the cast iron grid, flat side facing upwards.

METHOD

1. First, prepare the fish. Remove the spines from the John Dory and season with salt and olive oil.
2. For the juice: Using a mandolin, slice the apple and kohlrabi. You will need 3 slices of each, per serving.
3. Blanch the slices in boiling water for 5 seconds, before refreshing in iced water. Thoroughly drain.
4. In boiling water, blanch the parsley before refreshing in iced water.
5. Blend the parsley along with the water until vivid green.
6. Strain the mixture through a piece of clean cheesecloth.
7. Combine ¼ cup of the parsley water with ½ cup of apple/kohlrabi juice and season and thicken with optional cornstarch as needed.
8. To prepare the oyster cream, add the oysters along with the juice to the cream and warm for approximately 15 minutes.

9. Using a fine mesh sieve, strain while lightly pressing down on the oysters.

10. Remove the oysters and set to one side. You should yield approximately 2½ cup of the cream mixture.

11. Boil with the gelatin and set aside in the fridge to set.

12. Blend until creamy and smooth.

13. Cook the John Dory on the EGG and cook for 4 minutes each side.

14. Remove the fish to rest for a few minutes.

15. Arrange the oysters on the grid and cook for 5 minutes.

16. Shuck the oysters open and set the juice aside.

17. To serve: Put 6 dots of the oyster cream into 4 individual bowls.

18. Arrange 2 slices each of apple and kohlrabi on top. Garnish with the kohlrabi leaves.

19. Fillet the grilled John Dory and remove the skin.

20. Evenly divide the fish between the 4 individual bowls and top each one with a grilled oyster.

21. Add an additional slice of kohlrabi and apple on top of the John Dory.

22. Add a little of the kohlrabi, apple and parsley juice.

23. Garnish with herbs and wild, edible borage flowers.

LEMON AND ROSEMARY MARINATED GROUPER WITH TOMATO-BASIL SAUCE

(TOTAL COOK TIME 1 HOURS 20 MINS)

INGREDIENTS FOR 2 SERVINGS

THE FISH

- 2 grouper fillets

THE MARINADE

- Freshly squeezed lemon juice – 1 tablespoon
- Dried rosemary, crushed – ½ teaspoon
- Olive oil – 1½ teaspoons
- Salt – ¼ teaspoon
- Dash of black pepper

THE SAUCE

- Tomato, seeded, diced – ¼ cup
- Dried basil – 1 teaspoon
- Green onion, chopped – 1 tablespoon
- Red wine vinegar – 1 ½ teaspoon
- Orange peel, grated – ¼ teaspoon

THE GRILL

- Set the EGG for direct cooking to a temperature of 350°F (177°C)

METHOD

1. First, in a ziplock bag combine the fresh lemon juice with the rosemary, olive oil, salt, and black pepper.
2. Add the fish fillets to the bag.
3. Securely seal the ziplock bag and turn to evenly coat.
4. Transfer to the fridge for 60 minutes.
5. Drain and discard the marinade.
6. Arrange the fish on the perforated cooking grid and grill on both sides, until the fish fillets flake easily when using a fork.
7. In a pan, combine the sauce ingredients: tomato, basil, green onion, red wine vinegar, and orange peel and over moderate heat, cook until hot.
8. Serve the fish fillets with the sauce and enjoy.

CHAPTER-6 SEAFOOD

CRAB CAKES WITH SWEET BBQ RANCH DIPPING SAUCE

(TOTAL COOK TIME 30 MINUTES)

INGREDIENTS FOR 4 SERVINGS

THE SEAFOOD

- Canned lump crabmeat (1-lb, 0.45-kgs)

THE INGREDIENTS

- 2 large eggs, beaten
- 2 jalapenos, seeded, minced
- Panko breadcrumbs – ½ cup
- Mayonnaise – ½ cup
- Fresh parsley, chopped – 1 tablespoon
- Hot seasoning – 2 teaspoons

THE DIPPING SAUCE

- Sweet BBQ sauce, of choice – ½ cup
- Ranch dressing – ½ cup

THE GRILL

- For indirect cooking, set the EGG at 375°f (190°c)

METHOD

1. In a bowl, combine the eggs along with the jalapenos, breadcrumbs, mayonnaise, parsley, and hot seasoning. Stir to combine.
2. Add the crab meat to the mixture and using clean hands, gently combine.
3. Form the mixture into 4 evenly-sized balls, and using the palm of your hand, flatten them into 4 patty shapes.
4. Transfer to the EGG and cook for 18-20 minutes, until golden brown on both sides.
5. In a bowl, combine the BBQ sauce with the ranch dressing and use as a dip.
6. Serve and enjoy

OYSTER SPAGHETTI

(TOTAL COOK TIME 35 MINUTES)

INGREDIENTS FOR 4 SERVINGS

THE SEAFOOD

- 48 large oysters, shucked

THE INGREDIENTS

- Salted butter – 2 tablespoons
- Shallots, diced – ½ cup
- Green onion, white and green section, finely chopped – ¼ cup
- Garlic, peeled, chopped – 3 tablespoons
- Vermouth – 1 cup
- Heavy cream – 3 cups
- Fresh thyme, chopped – 1 tablespoon
- 1 bay leaf
- Spaghetti, cooked, drained (1-lb, 455-gms)
- Parmesan cheese, freshly grated – ½ cup

THE SMOKE

- Using a stir-fry pan and for direct cooking, set the EGG at 450°f (232°c)
- Use wood chips to give the dish a rich flavor

METHOD

1. In the pan, melt the butter.
2. Add the shallots and green onions to the pan and saute for 3 minutes, until translucent.
3. Turn the heat down to 375°F (191°C).
4. Add the garlic to the pan and fry for an additional 60 seconds.
5. Pour in the vermouth, swirling the pan to deglaze, and simmer for 2 minutes.
6. Add the oyster liquor along with the heavy cream, thyme, and bay leaf, and simmer for between 8-10 minutes, until the cream bubbles and the sauce reduces.
7. Stir in the grated cheese.
8. Add the oysters and cook until the edges are beginning to curl slightly.
9. Season to taste.
10. Add the drained pasta and cook until it is heated through.
11. Divide the cooked pasta along with the oysters into 6 individual pasta bowls.
12. Garnish with Parmesan and serve.

RED CHILI SCALLOPS WITH HOMEMADE SALSA

(TOTAL COOK TIME 25 MINUTES)

INGREDIENTS FOR 4 SERVINGS

THE SEAFOOD

- 12 large sea scallops
- Red chile rub, see recipe – 2 tablespoons

THE SALSA

- Fresh mango, pitted, diced – ¾ cup
- Red bell pepper, diced – ¼ cup
- Red onion, peeled, diced – ¼ cup
- Scallions, thinly sliced – ¼ cup
- Fresh mint, finely chopped – 2 tablespoons
- 1 garlic clove, peeled, crushed
- Freshly squeezed lime juice – 2 tablespoons
- Extra-virgin olive oil – 1 tablespoon
- Honey – 2 teaspoons
- Kosher salt – ½ teaspoon
- Freshly ground black pepper – ¼ tsp

THE RUB

- Cumin seed – 1 tablespoon
- Coriander seeds – 1 tablespoon
- Red chile flakes – 1 tablespoon
- Ancho chile powder – 1 tablespoon
- Kosher salt – 1 tablespoon
- Sweet paprika – 1 teaspoon
- Garlic powder – 1 teaspoon

THE GRILL

- Using the cast iron grid and for direct cooking, set the EGG at 500°F (260°c)

METHOD

1. To prepare the salsa: In a bowl and with a wooden spoon combine the mango with the red bell pepper, onion, scallions, mint, garlic, fresh lime juice, oil, honey, salt, and black pepper. Stir thoroughly and set to one side.

2. Generously season the scallops with the chili rub and arrange on the grid.

3. Close the EGG's lid and grill the scallops for approximately 2 minutes on each side, until just cooked and golden.

4. Transfer the cooked scallops to a serving platter.

5. When you are ready to assemble, arrange 3 scallops of each of the 4 plates.

6. Top with ¼ cup of the fresh salsa and serve.

7. To make the rub, on the stove top, in a small frying pan, toast the cumin seed along with the coriander and chili flakes for 5 minutes, or until the spices emit their fragrance. Remove the pan from the heat and set aside to cool.

8. Transfer the toasted mixture to a spice grinder and add the chili powder followed by the salt, paprika and garlic powder.

9. Grind the seasoning for between 15-20 seconds, until finely ground.

10. Store the rub in a resealable, airtight container until needed. This recipe yields ½ cup.

CHAPTER-7 CHICKEN

GREEK HERB ROASTED CHICKEN

(TOTAL COOK TIME 6 HOURS)

INGREDIENTS FOR 4-6 SERVINGS

THE MEAT

- 1 roasting chicken (3.5-lb, 1.6-kgs)

THE SEASONING

- Water – ¼ cup
- 2 chicken stock cubes
- Fresh lemon juice – ½ cup
- Lemon pepper seasoning - 1 tablespoon
- Canola oil – ½ cup
- Dried oregano – 1 tablespoon
- Zest of 1 medium lemon
- Fresh parsley, chopped – ¼ cup
- Beer/chicken stock, for roaster

THE GRILL

- After marinating, preheat your EGG to 350° F (177°C).

METHOD

1. First, prepare the seasoning. Add the water, stock cubes, lemon juice, lemon pepper seasoning, canola oil, oregano, lemon zest, and parsley to a blender and blitz until smooth.

2. Place the chicken in a stainless steel bowl and pour over the marinade. Turn the chicken to coat evenly. Chill for 4 hours, turning the chicken a few times during marinating.

3. Take the chicken out of the marinade and allow any excess to drip away.

4. Arrange the chicken on a vertical roaster and fill with beer or chicken stock. Arrange the vertical roaster inside a roasting tin to catch any drippings. Arrange on the cooking grid.

5. Cook until the breast meat registers an internal temperature of 165°F (75°C), approximately 1 hour.

6. Serve and enjoy.

RANCH-ROSEMARY CHICKEN KEBABS

(TOTAL COOK TIME 50 MINUTES)

INGREDIENTS FOR 6 SERVINGS

THE MEAT

- 5 boneless, skinless chicken breasts, cubed

THE MARINADE

- Ranch dressing – ½ cup
- Olive oil – ½ cup
- Fresh rosemary, minced – 1 tablespoon
- Worcestershire sauce – 3 tablespoons
- Lemon juice – 1 teaspoon
- Salt – 2 teaspoons
- Black pepper – ¼ teaspoon
- White vinegar – 1 teaspoon
- Sugar – 1 tablespoon

THE GRILL

- Preheat your EGG to 400° F (205°C) and prepare for direct cooking.

METHOD

1. Prepare the marinade. Combine the ranch dressing, olive oil, rosemary, Worcestershire sauce, lemon juice, salt, black pepper, vinegar, and sugar in a bowl. Allow to stand for several minutes.
2. Add the chicken and toss to coat. Chill for half an hour.
3. Thread the chicken cubes onto skewers and arrange on a lightly-oiled grid. Grill for approximately 10 minutes until white and cooked through.

SPANISH-SPICED BEER CAN CHICKEN

(TOTAL COOK TIME 6 HOURS)

INGREDIENTS FOR 6 SERVINGS

THE MEAT

- 1 whole chicken (5-lb, 2.25-kgs)
- Chorizo sausage, diced (5-oz, 140-gms)

THE MARINADE

- 1 can Spanish lager (14.8-oz, 440-ml)
- 1 dried ancho chili
- 1 small lime, sliced into wedges
- Whole black peppercorns, 1 teaspoon
- Sweet paprika – 1 teaspoon
- Cumin – ½ teaspoon
- Chili powder – ½ teaspoon
- Cayenne pepper – 1 teaspoon
- Granulated garlic – 1½ teaspoons
- Onion powder – 1½ teaspoons
- Sea salt – 2 tablespoons
- Black pepper – 1 tablespoon
- Olive oil – 2 tablespoons

THE SMOKE

- Preheat your EGG to 320° F (160°C) using apple wood.

METHOD

1. Open the can of lager and pour away half of the beer. Remove the ring pull and fill the can with the ancho chile, lime, and peppercorns. Shake the can gently to combine.

2. Using kitchen paper towels, pat the outside of the chicken dry. Stuff the diced chorizo under the chicken skin and into the neck area.

3. Next, combine the paprika, cumin, chili powder, cayenne pepper, garlic, onion, salt and black pepper in a small bowl. Rub the mixture onto the outside of the chicken. Arrange the filled beer can inside the carcass of the chicken and stand up in foil pan.

4. Arrange the chicken in the foil pan on the cooking grid and smoke for approximately 2½ hours until the meat registers an internal temperature of 165°F (75°C).

5. Take the chicken off the grill and remove the beer can. Allow the chicken to rest for 15 minutes before carving and serving.

CHAPTER-8 TURKEY

APPLE, BOURBON, AND BACON STUFFED TURKEY

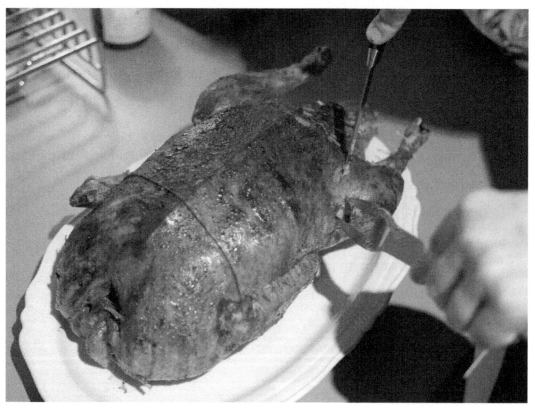

(TOTAL COOK TIME 5 HOURS 30 MINUTES)

INGREDIENTS FOR 12 SERVINGS

THE MEAT

- 1 whole turkey (11-lb, 5-kgs)

THE RUB

- Poultry rub – ¼ cup
- Melted butter – ¼ cup
- Bourbon – 2 tablespoons

THE STUFFING

- 2 jalapeno peppers, quartered
- 1 red onion, peeled and chopped
- 1 apple, chopped
- 5 garlic cloves, peeled and crushed
- Olive oil – ¼ cup
- 6 rashers bacon, chopped
- Black pepper – ¼ teaspoon
- Salt – 1 teaspoon
- Bourbon – 1 tablespoon
- Apple cider – 2 cups

THE SMOKE

- Arrange a cast-iron plate setter feet-up inside the EGG, close the lid and adjust the vents as necessary to get the temperature to 450° F (230°C).
- Soak smoke chips ready for later use.

METHOD

1. Rinse the turkey and then completely pat dry. Discard the next and giblets and place the bird in a roasting tin.
2. Combine the poultry rub, melted butter, and bourbon in a small bowl. Rub the mixture over the bird and under the breast skin.
3. In a second bowl, toss together the jalapeno peppers, red onion, apple, garlic cloves, olive oil, bacon, black pepper, salt, and bourbon.
4. Stuff half the mixture into the bird's cavity. Arrange the second half of the stuffing in a disposable aluminum tin and pour over the apple cider.
5. Place the disposable tin on the plate setter and arrange a grill rack over the top.
6. Arrange the turkey, breast down, on the grill rack. Close the lid and smoke for half an hour.
7. Open the lid and drop the soaked chips down the side of the smoker/grill through the gaps in the plate setter.
8. Flip the turkey over, close the lid, and bring the temperature down to 375°F (190°C). Cook until the meat registers an internal temperature of 165°F (75°C).
9. Transfer the turkey to a cutting board and loosely cover with aluminum foil. Allow to rest for 45 minutes before serving.

CLASSIC ROAST TURKEY

(TOTAL COOK TIME 4 HOURS 30 MINUTES)

INGREDIENTS FOR 8 SERVINGS

THE MEAT

- 1 whole turkey, cleaned (16-lb, 7.2-kgs)

THE INGREDIENTS

- Poultry seasoning
- 1 celery stalk
- 1 onion, peeled and halved
- Chicken broth – 2 cups

THE SMOKE

- Preheat the EGG to 325°F (165°C) using pecan chips and prepare for indirect cooking.

METHOD

1. Sprinkle the poultry seasoning all over the outside of the bird.
2. Arrange the bird on a vertical poultry roaster and arrange in a drip pan.
3. Add the celery and onion to the drip pan along with the chicken broth.
4. Cook the turkey until the meat registers an internal temperature of 165°F (75°C) approximately 3-4 hours.

TURKEY PARMIGIANA

(TOTAL COOK TIME 5 HOURS 30 MINUTES)

INGREDIENTS FOR 4-6 SERVINGS

THE MEAT

- Boneless turkey breast fillets (1-lb, 0.45-kgs)

THE INGREDIENTS

- 2 egg whites
- Water – 1 tablespoon
- Italian seasoned breadcrumbs – 2 tablespoons
- Parmesan cheese, grated – 2 tablespoons
- Marinara sauce – 1 cup
- Mozzarella cheese, shredded – 1 cup

THE GRILL

- Preheat the smoker/grill to 400°F (205°C) and prepare for indirect cooking.

METHOD

1. Whisk together the egg whites and water in a shallow dish.
2. In a second shallow dish, toss together the breadcrumbs and Parmesan.
3. Dip each turkey filet first in the egg white and then the breadcrumbs.
4. Arrange the meat in a pan and place on the cooking grid. Cook for half an hour.
5. Pour the marinara sauce over the breaded turkey and sprinkle over the mozzarella.
6. Cook for another 5 minutes until the cheese melts, and the turkey is write-through.

CHAPTER-9 GAME

CHERRY-SMOKED VENISON LOIN WITH PINK PEPPERCORNS

(TOTAL COOK TIME 35 MINUTES)

INGREDIENTS FOR 2-3 SERVINGS

THE GAME

- Loin of venison (1.3-lb, 0.6-kgs)

THE SEASONING

- Salt and black pepper
- Pinch of ground cumin

THE INGREDIENTS

- Almond oil – 4 tablespoons
- 1 shallot, chopped
- 1 garlic clove, peeled, sliced
- Pink peppercorns – 1 teaspoon
- Sesame seeds – 1 tablespoon
- 4 courgettes, sliced
- 3 fresh lemons

THE SMOKE

- For direct cooking using a cast iron searing grid set the EGG at 300°F (145°C).
- Use cherry wood chips (pre-soaked in water for 15 minutes).

METHOD

1. Season the venison with salt, pepper, and cumin.

2. Roast the venison on the grid, turning every 60-90 seconds until cooked to your preferred level of doneness, approximately 5-7 minutes.

3. In a pan, combine the oil with the shallots, garlic, pink peppercorns, and sesame seeds and heat through for 60 seconds.

4. Add the courgettes and on high heat, cook for 2 minutes. Drizzle in juice from the fresh lemons and serve alongside the venison.

CHILI-CRUSTED COLA WILD BOAR HAM

(TOTAL COOK TIME 4 HOURS 20 MINUTES)

INGREDIENTS FOR 6 SERVINGS

THE GAME

- 1 wild boar ham (3-lb, 1.36-kgs)
- 1 regular-size can of cola, any brand

THE SEASONING

- Chili powder (6-ozs, 170-gms)
- Granulated garlic – 1 tablespoon
- Onion powder – 1 tablespoon
- Cumin – 2 tablespoons
- Dark brown sugar – 4 tablespoons

THE GRILL

- For indirect cooking set the EGG at 300°F (145°C)

METHOD

1. Add the boar to a drip pan.
2. In a bowl combine the seasoning mix ingredients: chili powder, granulated garlic, onion powder, cumin, and dark brown sugar. Mixing until entirely combined.
3. Pat, the seasoning mix all over the boar, liberally covering it on all its sides.
4. Pour the cola into the pan but not over the boar.
5. Cover tightly with aluminum foil.
6. Put the pan on the cooking grid and bake until tender, for 4 hours. Do not open or remove the foil while the meat cooks.
7. Remove the meat from the EGG and set aside to cool before shredding and serving.

SMOKED DUCK BREAST WITH FRUIT

(TOTAL COOK TIME 1 HOURS 20 MINS)

INGREDIENTS FOR 2 SERVINGS

THE GAME

- 2 duck breasts

THE INGREDIENTS

- Salt and black pepper
- 2 ripe oranges, whole
- Handful of ripe plums pitted, halved

THE SMOKE

- Preheat your EGG for indirect cooking to 220°F (110°C).
- The plate setter must be in the legs up position. Position the stainless steel grid on the top of the plate setter legs
- When you are ready to cook, drain the water from the wood chips, and remove the plate setter.
- In a large circle, scatter the wood chips onto the charcoal.
- Replace the plate setter along with the stainless steel grid.

METHOD

1. Using kitchen paper towel, pat the duck dry

2. Using a sharp knife, score the duck's skin

3. Season the duck with salt, and black pepper and grate the orange zest over the duck breasts

4. Position the duck on the stainless steel grid, skin side upwards

5. Arrange the plums, cut side facing down on the grid

6. Place the whole 2 oranges on the grid

7. Close the lid to the EGG and cook for 40-45 minutes

8. Open and burp the lid

9. The duck is sufficiently cooked when an internal thermometer registers a temperature of 165° F (75°C)

10. Remove the duck from the EGG and set aside to rest for 10 minutes.

11. Thinly slice the duck and squeeze the orange from the juice over the top.

12. Serve with the plums and enjoy.

CHAPTER-10 VEGGIES

DOUBLE-SMOKED BACON STUFFED POTATOES

(TOTAL COOK TIME 1 HOUR 50 MINUTES)

INGREDIENTS FOR 4 SERVINGS

THE VEGETABLES

- 4 large baking potatoes, scrubbed, dried, pierced several times

THE STUFFING

- 4 slices bacon, cut crosswise into 0.2-ins (0.62-cms) pieces
- Scallions, finely chopped – 4 tablespoons
- Cheddar cheese, coarsely grated – 2 cups
- Sour cream – ½ cup
- Unsalted butter, cold, thinly sliced – 4 tablespoons
- Smoked paprika, to season

THE POTATO INGREDIENTS

- Butter, melted – 2 tablespoons
- Coarse sea salt
- Freshly ground black pepper

THE SMOKE

- For indirect cooking, set the EGG to 450°F (232°C).
- Preheat a griddle, ridged side facing upwards.
- After cooking the bacon, remove the grid and add 2-3 chunks of hardwood.
- Turn the head down to 400°F (205°C).

METHOD

1. Add the bacon to the pan and cook until crispy. Remove from the EGG and put to one side.

2. Brush the washed, dried and pierced potatoes with melted butter and generously season.

3. Arrange the potatoes on the EGG grid and roast for between 60-90 minutes, until fork tender.

4. Transfer the potatoes to a chopping board. Slice each of the potatoes in half lengthwise. While still a little hot, carefully scrape out the majority of the potato flesh, leaving a ¼ -ins (0.62-cms) shell.

5. Coarsely mash the flesh, until chunky and transfer to a bowl. Stir in the scallions, cheddar cheese, sour cream, and cooked bacon.

6. Stuff the potato mixture into the potato skins, heaping it in the middle.

7. Dot each potato with a slice of butter and garnish with paprika.

8. When you are ready to serve, reheat the stuffed potatoes in the preheated EGG at 400°F (204°C) for between 20-25 minutes, until bubbling and brown.

9. Serve.

MASHED SMOKED AUBERGINE

(TOTAL COOK TIME 1 HOUR 50 MINUTES)

INGREDIENTS FOR 4-6 SERVINGS

THE VEGETABLES

- 2 aubergines

THE INGREDIENTS

- Tahini – 3 tablespoons
- Fresh lemon juice – 1 tablespoon
- 1-2 garlic cloves, peeled
- Flat leaf parsley, roughly chopped – 2 tablespoons
- Flaky sea salt – ½ teaspoon
- Black pepper – ¼ teaspoon
- Olive oil – 2 tablespoons
- Pomegranate arils, to garnish – 1 tablespoon
- Flatbread, warm, to serve

THE SMOKE

- Heat the EGG to 225°F (116°C)

METHOD

1. Prick each aubergine a few times with the sharp tip of a knife. This will prevent them from exploding.
2. Arrange them on the stainless steel grid and blacken, while turning every 5-10 minutes, until entirely charred. This will take between 20-25 minutes.
3. Remove the aubergines from the EGG and set aside to rest for 10-15 minutes.
4. When the aubergine is sufficiently cool to handle, lengthwise split the aubergines. Scoop out the aubergine flesh, and discard their skins.
5. In a bowl, combine the tahini with the fresh lemon juice, garlic, and parsley.
6. Gently mash the aubergines with a fork until a chunky texture.
7. Stir the aubergine into the tahini-parsley mixture and season.
8. Arrange on a platter, drizzle with oil and garnish with pomegranate arils.
9. Serve with warmed flatbread and enjoy.

TRIO OF MUSHROOM SALAD WITH TOMATO PERSILLADE

(TOTAL COOK TIME 1 HOUR 55 MINUTES)

INGREDIENTS FOR 4 SERVINGS

THE VEGETABLES

- Shitake mushrooms (8-ozs, 227-gms)
- Oyster mushrooms (8-ozs, 227-gms)
- Portabella mushrooms (8-ozs, 227-gms)

THE INGREDIENTS

- Kosher salt – 1 tablespoon
- Freshly ground black pepper – 1 tablespoon
- Extra-virgin olive oil – ½ cup
- Baby spinach (8-ozs,227-gms)
- Arugula (8-ozs,227-gms)
- 8 rashers of cooked bacon
- Goat cheese, crumbled – ½ cup

THE PERSILLADE

- 4 Roma tomatoes, chopped
- Flat-leaf parsley, chopped – ½ cup
- 4 garlic cloves, peeled
- Freshly squeezed lemon juice – 3 tablespoons
- Kosher salt – 1 tablespoon
- Ground black pepper – 1 tablespoon

THE SMOKE

- Heat the EGG for indirect cooking to 325°F (163°C)
- Use hickory wood smoke chips

METHOD

1. Toss the mushrooms in salt, and black pepper, then the oil and transfer to a ziplock bag. Set aside for 60 minutes, to marinate.
2. Remove the mushrooms from the ziplock bag and arrange on the cooking grid.
3. In the EGG, smoke the mushrooms for 25 minutes.
4. Remove and set to one side.
5. To build the salad, in a bowl, combine the spinach with the arugula.
6. Thinly slice the portabella mushroom. Roll each thin slice and lay on the bed of mixed greens.
7. On either side of the rolls, arrange the shitake mushrooms.
8. Place the oyster mushrooms on top.
9. Crumbed the cooked bacon over the mushrooms and scatter with the goat cheese crumbles.
10. To prepare the persillade, in a blender or processor pulse the tomatoes along with the parsley, garlic, fresh lemon juice, salt, and black pepper.
11. A little at a time, drizzle in the olive oil.
12. Drizzle with the persillade and enjoy.

CHAPTER-11 SMOKING TIPS AND TRICKS

Before starting the recipes, let's discuss a few tips and tricks about smoking meats.

SELECTING A SMOKER

You need to invest in a good smoker if you are going to smoke meat on a regular basis. Consider these options when buying a smoker. Here are two natural fire option for you:

- Charcoal smokers are fueled by a combination of charcoal and wood. Charcoal burns easily and the temperature remains steady, so you won't have any problem with a charcoal smoker. The wood gives a great flavor to the meat and you will enjoy smoking meats.

- Wood smoker: The wood smoker will give your brisket and ribs the best smoky flavor and taste, but it is a bit harder to cook with wood. Both hardwood blocks and chips are used as fuel.

CHOOSE YOUR WOOD

You need to choose your wood carefully because the type of wood you will use affect greatly to the flavor and taste of the meat. Here are a few options for you:

- Maple: Maple has a smoky and sweet taste and goes well with pork or poultry

- Alder: Alder is sweet and light. Perfect for poultry and fish.

- Apple: Apple has a mild and sweet flavor. Goes well with pork, fish, and poultry.

- Oak: Oak is great for slow cooking. Ideal for game, pork, beef, and lamb.

- Mesquite: Mesquite has a smoky flavor and extremely strong. Goes well with pork or beef.

- Hickory: Has a smoky and strong flavor. Goes well with beef and lamb.

- Cherry Has a mild and sweet flavor. Great for pork, beef, and turkey

To cook the meat, you may refer the below-mentioned chart that can help you with selecting the best wood chips/chunks

Wood Type	Fish	Chicken	Beef	Pork
Apple	Yes	Yes	No	No
Alder	Yes	Yes	No	Yes
Cherry	Yes	Yes	Yes	Yes
Hickory	No	No	Yes	Yes
Maple	No	Yes	No	No
Mulberry	Yes	Yes	No	Yes
Mesquite	No	No	Yes	Yes
Oak	Yes	Yes	Yes	Yes
Pecan	No	Yes	Yes	Yes
Pear	No	Yes	No	Yes
Peach	No	Yes	No	Yes
Walnut	No	No	Yes	Yes

Remember, black smoke is bad and white smoke is good. Ensure proper ventilation for great tasting smoked meat.

SELECT THE RIGHT MEAT

Some meats are just ideal for the smoking process, including:

- Chicken

- Turkey

- Pork roast

- Ham

- Brisket

- Pork and beef ribs

- Corned beef

FIND THE RIGHT TEMPERATURE

- Start at 250F (120C): Start your smoker a bit hot. This extra heat gets the smoking process going.

- Temperature drop: Once you add the meat to the smoker, the temperature will drop, which is fine.

- Maintain the temperature. Monitor and maintain the temperature. Keep the temperature steady during the smoking process.

Avoid peeking every now and then. Smoke and heat two most important element make your meat taste great. If you open the cover every now and then you lose both of them and your meat loses flavor. Only the lid only when you truly need it.

THE CORE DIFFERENCE BETWEEN COLD AND HOT SMOKING

Depending on the type of grill that you are using, you might be able to get the option to go for a Hot Smoking Method or a Cold Smoking One. The primary fact about these three different cooking techniques which you should keep in mind are as follows:

- **Hot Smoking:** In this technique, the food will use both the heat on your grill and the smoke to prepare your food. This method is most suitable for items such as chicken, lamb, brisket etc.
- **Cold Smoking:** In this method, you are going to smoke your meat at a very low temperature such as 30 degree Celsius, making sure that it doesn't come into the direct contact with the heat. This is mostly used as a means to preserve meat and extend their life on the shelf.
- **Roasting Smoke:** This is also known as Smoke Baking. This process is essentially a combined form of both roasting and baking and can be performed in any type of smoker with a capacity of reaching temperatures above 82 degree Celsius.

THE BASIC PREPARATIONS

- Always be prepared to spend the whole day and take as much time as possible to smoke your meat for maximum effect.
- Make sure to obtain the perfect Ribs/Meat for the meal which you are trying to smoke. Do a little bit of research if you need.
- I have already added a list of woods in this book, consult to that list and choose the perfect wood for your meal.
- Make sure to prepare the marinade for each of the meals properly. A great deal of the flavor comes from the rubbing.
- Keep a meat thermometer handy to get the internal temperature when needed.
- Use mittens or tongs to keep yourself safe
- Refrain yourself from using charcoal infused alongside starter fluid as it might bring a very unpleasant odor to your food
- Always make sure to start off with a small amount of wood and keep adding them as you cook.
- Don't be afraid to experiment with different types of wood for newer flavor and experiences.
- Always keep a notebook near you and note jot down whatever you are doing or learning and use them during the future session. This will help you to evolve and move forward.

THE CORE ELEMENTS OF SMOKING!

Smoking is a very indirect method of cooking that relies on a number of different factors to give you the most perfectly cooked meal that you are looking for. Each of these components is very important to the whole process as they all work together to create the meal of your dreams.

- **Time**: Unlike grilling or even Barbequing, smoking takes a really long time and requires a whole lot of patience. It takes time for the smoky flavor to slowly get infused into the meats. Jus to bring things into comparison, it takes an about 8 minutes to fully cook a steak through direct heating, while smoking (indirect heating) will take around 35-40 minutes.

- **Temperature:** When it comes to smoking, the temperature is affected by a lot of different factors that are not only limited to the wind, cold air temperatures but also the cooking wood's dryness. Some smokers work best with large fires that are controlled by the draw of a chimney and restricted airflow through the various vents of the cooking chamber and firebox. While other smokers tend to require smaller fire with fewer coals as well as a completely different combination of the vent and draw controls. However, most smokers are designed to work at temperatures as low as 180 degrees Fahrenheit to as high as 300 degrees Fahrenheit. But the recommend temperature usually falls between 250 degrees Fahrenheit and 275 degrees Fahrenheit.

- **Airflow:** The level of air to which the fire is exposed to greatly determines how your fire will burn and how quickly it will burn the fuel. For instance, if you restrict air flow into the firebox by closing up the available vents, then the fire will burn at a low temperature and vice versa. Typically in smokers, after lighting up the fire, the vents are opened to allow for maximum airflow and is then adjusted throughout the cooking process to make sure that optimum flame is achieved.

- **Insulation:** Insulation is also very important when it comes to smokers as it helps to easily manage the cooking process throughout the whole cooking session. A good insulation allows smokers to efficiently reach the desired temperature instead of waiting for hours upon hours!

CONCLUSION

The book includes smoked meat recipes comprising beef, fish, seafood, pork, poultry, vegetables, and game. If you want to just treat yourself to mouthwatering, perfectly cooked smoked meat or entertain family or friends, this book will provide everything you need.

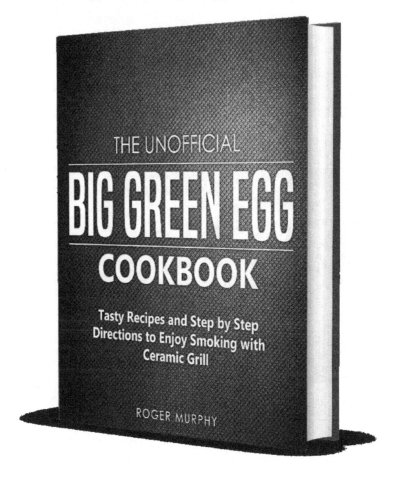

MY BOOKS

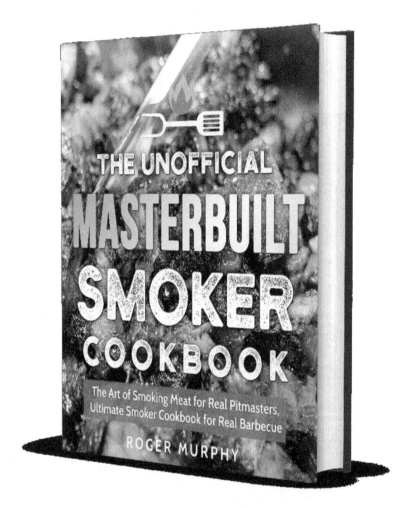

https://www.amazon.com/dp/1797805525

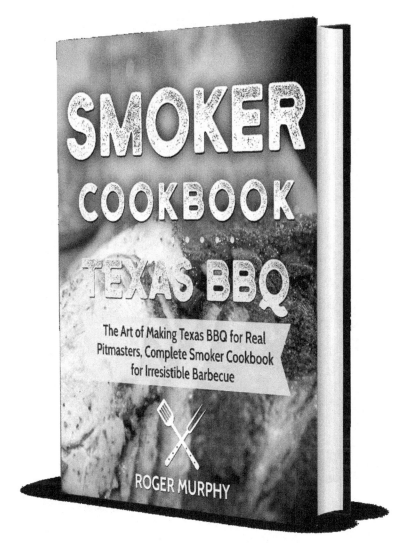

https://www.amazon.com/dp/1796455032

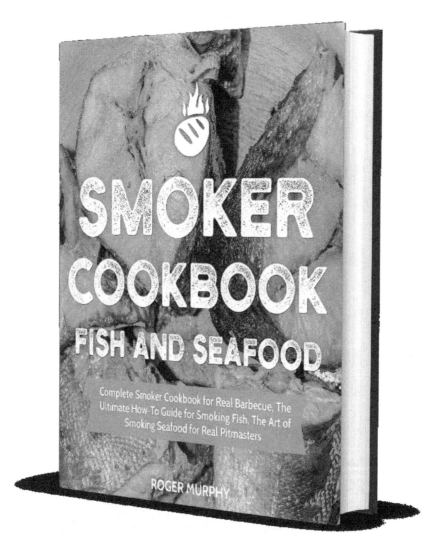

https://www.amazon.com/dp/1790806062

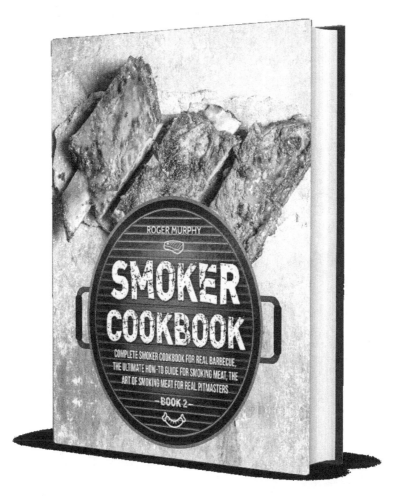

https://www.amazon.com/dp/B07KYWLF13

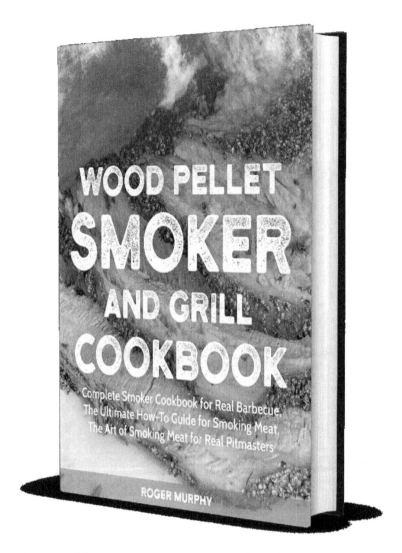

https://www.amazon.com/dp/1731126360

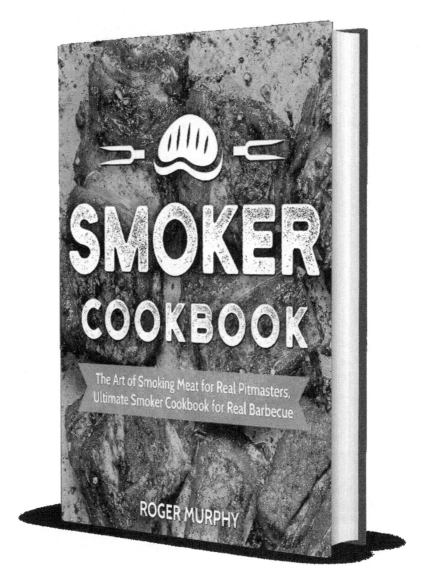

https://www.amazon.com/dp/1731563310

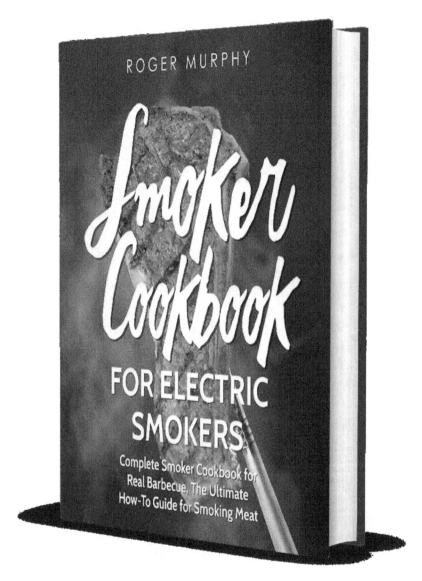

https://www.amazon.com/dp/1790442931

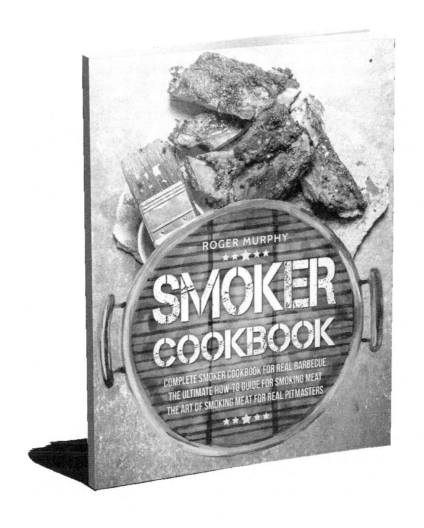

https://www.amazon.com/dp/1981340289

P.S. Thank you for reading this book. If you've enjoyed this book, please don't shy, drop me a line, leave a feedback or both on Amazon. I love reading feedbacks and your opinion is extremely important for me.

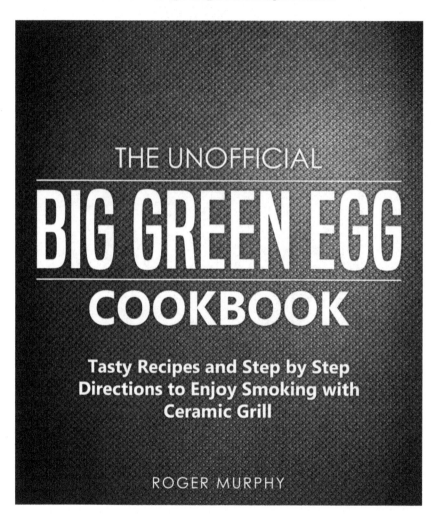

GET YOUR FREE GIFT

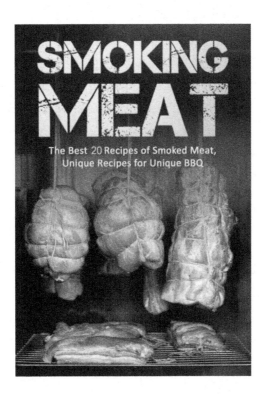

Subscribe to our Mail List and get your FREE copy of the book

'Smoking Meat: The Best 20 Recipes of Smoked Meat, Unique Recipes for Unique BBQ'

https://tiny.cc/smoke20

Copyright 2019© Roger Murphy

Made in the USA
Columbia, SC
14 June 2019